C

SHIFT

Growing Your Capacity

Through Confidence

KENNETH KALLEN

This book is for me. It is the most selfish thing I have ever done. In order to accomplish anything great, we all have to be a little more selfish. We need to learn to take care of ourselves first. This book is my guidebook, to remind myself that, in order for me to serve others with my best ability, I must take care of myself first.

That being said, humans need other humans in order to achieve extraordinary things. There have been many extraordinary humans in my life whom I would like to thank for being a part of my journey. I appreciate all of you, and all you have and continue to inspire me to keep growing my capacity!

To my wife. My hummingbird. You are my person. I am constantly pushed and challenged by you to grow my capacity as a human. I am the luckiest man on Earth. Not many women would let their husband take a year-long journey to coach his dream job three months before we got married. But you knew I needed to keep pushing myself, to find out what I am capable of. I now know I am capable of incredible things, but the two of us together are bound for extraordinary things!

To my parents. You do not get to choose your parents. I won the parent lottery. Both my parents provided an environment for me to be curious, to play, and to explore. They never pushed me to do anything I didn't want to do, but if I made a commitment, they made me honor it. Most people do not want to grow up and be like their parents. I hope I am exactly like mine.

To Ken Vick and Velocity Sports Performance. Thank you for taking me from obese intern to a coach for professional athletes and Olympians. For giving me the tools and resources to be the best coach I could be.

To my mentors:

AJ Mihrzad, for teaching me to attract, sell, and serve like a million-dollar online super-coach, and for getting me to write this book in one weekend at his house.

Danny Rios, Mike Bledsoe, and the Strong Coach Program, for teaching me to be unreasonable. For lighting a fire inside me to want not to heal the fitness industry but to create what is next.

Carl Paoli, for inspiring me to be a better coach and a better human. Convincing me that my message and my story needed to be heard. Also, for helping me in my darkest days, to help me see the light and make it through!

Finally, to you, the reader. This book is not a book. It is an experience. The only way you get anything out of this book is if you actually get up and take action. The problem with society today is we mistake *thinking* about doing something for actually *doing* something. This book, if you take action and develop your process, will transform your life. But you have to actually get up and do it!

CONTENTS

FOREWORD

I FIRST MET KENNY after he applied for a mentorship program I was offering. What caught my attention about him was that he had a dream job. He was an Olympic-level action-sports coach. I soon realized Kenny was much more than that.

I admire Kenny for having the courage to acknowledge he was struggling to find clarity in his life when he first reached out to me. I am honored he chose me to guide him through the transition from being an action sports coach to now coaching other coaches and becoming the author of this book, which is designed to help us make the shift we need to find clarity and grow into our own potential.

I believe the best coaches are the best students—students who have a passion for sharing what they've learned with the intention of helping others get their needs met and thrive. Coaches are individuals who are able to lead people to higher levels of performance through simple yet effective practice, insightful conversation, inspiration, and presenting their students with a never-ending challenge designed to meet them where they are and stretch their current capacity. This is who Coach Kenny is. Now he will be for you, too, throughout the pages of this book.

Developing clarity to gain the confidence needed to make the best decisions and take the right action toward growth has been the theme of Kenny's life. Now he has gifted this process to us, by translating his experience into a simple and clear manual, so we can do the same for ourselves.

Think of this book as a roadmap to create a new mental model that will help you uncover the potential in all aspects of your life and, over time, allow you to become who you've always desired to be. You.

Enjoy the shift,

Carl Paoli, Founder
free+style connection

INTRODUCTION

THIS IS KIND OF HARD for me to share, because of who I am: a coach. But I struggle with confidence and self-esteem.

Even as I sit down to write this book, as the words come out of my mouth, as I hear them pass through my ears and into my brain, they sound terrible. Like no one is going to understand me or I am I. Why are people going to care about *me*?

Confidence is something I've struggled with my entire life. Why is that? It comes from when I was younger. You see, when I was a kid, I was really blind. I had one eye smaller than the other, so I had to cover one eye to strengthen the muscles of the weaker eye. In order to do that, I had to wear a pirate patch over my eye.

While that might sound really cool to do, as a kid, it was actually pretty traumatic. I still believe it stunted my development. With glasses on, you are unable to see things and perceive the world as you think you should or the way everyone else sees the world.

Then there's the social aspect of growing up as a kid who wore glasses. It may sound just funny and awkward, but when you're the only person who looks that way, it really hurts a kid's confidence and self-esteem. I was the only person like that. The person always called the four-eyes or nerd.

Now I understand how these unique problems, growing, is something a lot of people—maybe everybody!—deals with. For a lot of us, we feel there is something wrong with them.

Since I wasn't going to be the best-looking kid, in order to fit in, I decided I was going to be either the most athletic or the funniest kid around. I wanted people to remember me for something other than glasses.

I became determined to be the smartest. The most athletic. The most liked. I focused all my energy into creating every one of these talents. I had to try very hard, so I could be the best I could in all those areas, because I was the kid who wore glasses, who was the dork.

So, as the kid with the glasses who was a dork, I was always trying harder. In sports, I wanted to be the fastest. I wanted to be the strongest. At school, I wanted to be the smartest and funniest. This became my way to find out how I would fit in.

Sports, reading, math, science, and being funny: this became who I was. I really loved baseball when I was a kid. I was catcher, which doesn't make sense for someone with glasses, but I wasn't gonna let anything past me. I was going to be the fastest kid back there behind the plate, and I wasn't going to let anyone steal any bases.

I did not allow what I thought of as my disability to affect my performance or my confidence. My glasses were not going to stop me from doing the things I loved. I found ways to fit in, whether it be sports or academics. As a result, as a teenager, I got really good at sports and school. They were my thing.

For the five years I played Little League, my team went to the championship game every year, but for five years in a row, I came in second place.

This was a huge blow to a kid's confidence. To a kid who is trying to be the best they can be in everything, when you're denied winning, it's hard. All I really wanted to do was be the best, since that's what I thought I needed to be, to fit in with everyone.

A similar thing happened when I went into high school. I finally got contacts and ditched the glasses. I suddenly felt a lot more confident about how I looked.

Getting contacts and feeling good about how I looked improved my performance. Look good, feel good. It was a total game-changer for me. I got rid of the glasses, changed my haircut, and it changed my identity. I was no longer the four-eyed kid.

After I got contacts, my high school football team didn't lose any games until my junior year. We were a very good team—not the biggest guys, but we were faster than everyone else and we played as a team. We wanted it more than the other teams.

During my senior year, we even went to the championship and played at Angels Stadium for the CIF Southern Section State Championships. We played under the lights on the big field and, unfortunately, got our asses handed to us. We got spanked. My one claim to fame is that, on that day, I tackled future-NFL Quarterback Marc Sanchez!

But still, I never really was able to put everything together and be that winner I wanted to be.

Then, when I went to college, it was a brand-new environment. I could be anyone I wanted to be, because everyone was new. However, I still tried to fit in. Again, I thought I needed to be that person whom everybody liked.

So, like most college freshmen, I turned to drinking. Drinking became my new thing. Playing beer pong, winning, partying, and having a good time. After four years of college, when I graduated, I had ballooned up to this huge 250-260-pound person.

I wasn't able to get a job. Like everyone says, go to college, get a job. Well, it doesn't quite work out that way. So again, I had issues with my confidence. Where would I be accepted and fit in?

Since I was not able to get a job, I had to suck it up. I packed my bags and moved back home with Mom and Dad, where I finally found an internship at a place called Velocity Sports Performance. This is where I first got my start.

On the first day of my internship, I had to fill in for a coach who called in sick. I've never looked back since then. I taught kids how to run, how to work out, how to lift, and how to get strong. I was the coach who helped other high school athletes get scholarships.

During my internship, I discovered lifting. Lifting weights really changed my life. It's one of those things you do every day, even when you're not good at it. You do get better at it as you go, and it teaches you how to be strong.

It also gives you a lot of confidence. The first time I deadlifted three hundred pounds, when the bar came back to the ground, it shook the earth. And something inside me shifted. *Whoa!* I did that! It was the most powerful feeling I had ever felt, and I was hooked. From there on in, I lifted everything I saw. I read everything I could. And I signed up for a powerlifting meet.

When I competed in my first powerlifting meet, finally I *won*. It was such an incredible feeling. Finally, I had won something. I had found something that was for me, and that I could feel good about. Confident. I also finally felt like I had overcome all of those issues of self-esteem that I'd been struggling with. The key was finding something truly unique to me that I feel good about every day.

I spent the next ten years of my life working on becoming the best coach I could be.

That's why I'm writing this book: to help bring awareness to everybody. To say, Hey, everybody has obstacles they have to overcome. Not everyone's life is as perfect as it looks on Instagram or Facebook. You only see the highlights. You don't see the setbacks and the struggles.

I hope this book inspires you, too, to be the best you can be and not try to be what others want you to be.

This book is the most selfish thing I have ever done. This book is for me, as a reminder to bring more joy into my life. I've struggled with self-confidence my whole life, even throughout my career as a coach. I have coached athletes from age four years old all the way up to Olympians. I know what it takes to succeed at the highest level. However, I have struggled with fear, anxiety, depression, and obesity, personally. I had to overcome each of these things, and in overcoming them, I developed my process for finding joy.

That was the answer. I had worked in the fitness industry my entire life. I had given everything to it. I wanted to be the best coach, so my clients would receive extraordinary results.

But I cared so much about my clients, I stopped caring about myself. I stopped enjoying what I was doing. I became depressed, I gained thirty-five pounds, and I stayed in a hostile environment for a long time. I started to resent and hate being a coach. There I was, giving all of myself to my athletes and having them not care as much as I did. My whole life was about helping my athletes reach the highest level of performance, and it started breaking me.

This happens to all of us at some point. We just want to quit. It feels like everything is against us and, no matter what we try to do, we cannot win. I know because I've been there. I never thought I would be depressed—I'm someone who has been happy my whole life. But I stopped investing in me. I stopped growing. And when you stop growing, you start dying.

That is the reason for writing this book. To give you hope. To show you how to come out of your darkest days stronger and better than ever before.

It starts with building confidence. When we have confidence, we can increase our capacity. The more capacity we have, the harder we are to kill. I knew, inside me, I had the capacity to help others reach their dreams at the highest level. But I needed to invest those skills into myself. I needed to come up with my process for confidence.

As a coach, I know that programs work for four to six weeks. So, for myself, I did not want a program that just got me results. Results do not matter. We cannot control the results. We can miss our flight.

There can be bad weather. The other person can have a good day. We can have a bad day. Results are out of our control.

We must focus on what we can control: *our process*. We can control our process.

I became committed to create *my* process. A process that brought joy back into my life. I had lived in gyms, trying to become the best coach I could be, for a full ten years. Now, I wanted a new fitness experience. I wanted to find a way to enjoy the process. I knew, if I enjoyed the process, then the result wouldn't matter, because I would enjoy the person I became in the process. That is what we can control. That's how we show up every day.

This book is my framework for creating my process for confidence, so I can continue to grow my capacity. I use science, intuition, and joy to combat stress, and to increase efficiency, energy, intuition, and creativity. I want to teach people how to create and live their perfect day every day.

 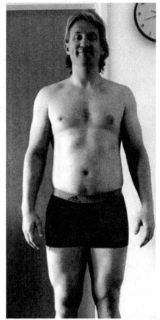

I do that by showing you how to create your own process for confidence, to increase your energy, adaptation, and motivation, which will allow you to have more creativity, intuition, and joy. To live your perfect day every day.

We all have our own stories to tell.

We cannot have a perfect day every day. The people who are successful have invested the time needed into creating their process. So, when they do have a bad day, their process catches them and prevents them from having two bad days in a row.

We build confidence by celebrating wins each day, no matter how small. Win or lose. Each day we celebrate a win, we start to build momentum. Momentum builds confidence. Confidence allows you to grow your capacity to overcome challenges and live your perfect day every day.

The book is structured as a process, the process I use as a coach to grow my athletes' capacity and close the learning loop.

In every session with my athletes, my goal is to have an "*A-ha* Moment." That's the moment when their eyes get very big and bright, and the lightbulb in their head goes off. They have finally shifted and understand what they need to do.

The technical name for this is a **Cognitive Shift.** It's a new experience that causes us to change the way we think. It's when we have a tremendous insight or breakthrough, we finally remove what has been holding us back, and we are now able to grow our capacity.

This is such an incredible moment for both coach and athlete. I live for these moments, because it is what allows my athletes to have their best performances. I want my athletes to be better than me. To know all of the things I know now that I wish I'd known when I was an athlete.

STRUCTURE:

CARE, TEACH, TRAIN, APPLY

I'VE STRUCTURED THIS book the same way I structure my class. This structure facilitates or allows for these "A-ha Moments" to happen. Structure and processes allow for predictable, repeatable, reliable results.

In order for you to change, you have to change your mind. This book offers a framework and structure for how I created my process.

Like everyone, you are unique. Your process will be different from anyone else's. Take what structure I give you here and apply it to your life. The sooner you apply what you read and learn from this book, the sooner you will start to transform. Your transformation is dependent on your speed of implementation.

Care: "People do not care how much you know, until they know how much you care."

Going forward, I start each chapter with a story. These stories come from my year coaching the Chinese National Ski Halfpipe team. I was the fitness coach for the ski halfpipe team, part of Team China getting ready for the 2022 Olympics in Beijing.

I do not speak Chinese or ski very well, but I was their fitness coach, so it was my job to make sure that their nine athletes did not get hurt and were improving their performance in the halfpipe. My goal was to develop the confidence of these nine Chinese athletes so they could maximize their abilities to compete at the highest level.

That is how I know this structure works. I have tested it on athletes who do not even speak my language! If I was able to build their confidence enough to place three girls into the Top 10 in the world in their sport, then I *know* it will work for you.

The most important part of the process is this: We have to show others we care. That is evident in these stories about how my young athletes learned to be confident and compete at the highest level. All they needed was for me to believe in them, so they could believe in themselves.

So, the first part of every chapter here is to remind ourselves, if we are going to serve anyone else or help anyone else, we must take care of ourselves first. We cannot fill others up from an empty cup. We must learn to fill our cup up first and then pour from an overflowing cup. We must learn to be a little selfish and take care of our needs before those of others. Saying yes to someone else is saying no to ourselves. If you do that for too long, you will not like where you end up. Unfortunately, others will keep taking until you have nothing left to give.

Teach: This is the second section of each chapter. In it, we look to science for answers.

Science has been guiding us for centuries. However, science is not the truth. Science is the *pursuit* of truth. Science, more often than not, gives us a range of what works for most people.

In these parts of the book, we will look at what some of the most famous scientists have said in the areas of: learning, energy, adaptation, and motivation. This will help us to start to build our own processes. Science is the pursuit of truth, but it is not the truth. We must look at science to see what is out there, but then use our intuition and creativity to discover out what is best for us and what bring us the most joy.

Train: This is where we grow our capacity.

In order to overcome challenges, we must keep increasing our capacity. I suggest hiring a coach to help you grow your capacity.

I define coaching as: growing your capacity. It is an inside out process. We must look inside first.

➢ What is it we are curious about?
➢ What programs exist out there that spark our curiosity or interest?
➢ What looks fun?

> ➢ What coaches are doing cool things?

This is where we get to explore and feel like a kid again.

There are many "fitness" programs out there for everyone, and new ones are being created constantly. Go out there and pick one. Try it out. See how it goes. What results did you get?

In order for us to become the person we want to be, we have to take action and actually train our body. That is how we grow our capacity, by constantly exposing it to new and novel stimuli, so we can adapt.

That is the essence of training: our body learning to adapt to pressure and tension (stress).

Apply: This is where you get to use your creativity and intuition to create your own process.

It is good to try out other people's programs. But most programs are built to fit the masses. That is what is wrong with the fitness industry.

We look at all of these fit people and ask them, "What diet are you doing?" "What workouts are you doing?" "Lose ten pounds in ten days?—perfect!"

This is all great, but each of those programs was designed for a specific person in order to get a specific result. That person got *their* results. Now, you want *your* results.

We must first figure out what it is we are excited about and interested in. Then, we can take action on it. If we are not excited about a program or exercise strategy, we will stop following it as soon as it becomes difficult. It is not just about following a program for six weeks, anyway. It is about finding a way to shift our thinking, so we change our behavior.

Behavior change is not easy.

Start putting this program into practice. Speed of implementation is the key to transformation, followed closely by seeking feedback.

Get feedback from the results. Win or learn. At first, our process will be terrible. But, in time, we will optimize it to get better and better, so we keep playing with it until it gets us predicable, reliable, repeatable results.

We want to create our own process so we can always be striving to maximize our potential. You will find that our potential is limited only by our thinking.

Once we have our process dialed in and working, we can just insert ourselves into any new environment and reach any goal we set for ourselves, because we have mastered our energy, our adaptation, and our motivation. That is what we want out of life: the confidence to go into any environment and know we will be successful because our process is bulletproof.

###

This book is my process, the one that has worked for me. Try it. Keep what works. Disregard what doesn't. Add other things from other places.

In fact, that is how I put this together. I stole other ideas from other coaches and discovered what worked for me. I then tweaked it a little and put my own style and flavor on it, so it is uniquely my process.

I trust my process, because I have invested the time into creating it. Now, it creates whatever I want, because I have optimized my lifestyle.

I know this book works. I proved it to myself and then I went out and proved it by coaching that team of Chinese athletes to become the best in the world at their sport, without speaking their language or even knowing their sport! The trick was I showed them I cared about them. I showed them how to care for themselves.

You cannot be a good athlete if you are not first a healthy human. When you start caring about yourself and loving yourself in the way only you know how to do, your life opens up to all of the opportunity and possibility you can ever imagine.

Create your process, live your perfect day every day.

We often mistake *thinking* about doing something for actually *doing*. But if it exists in your head, it doesn't exist at all.

Emotion = Energy in motion

If you do not like your current emotion, get up and move. We are not trees stuck into the ground.

This book teaches you how to take back personal responsibility for your life. This is not a book, really. It is an experience. Express yourself.

CHAPTER 1

A PROCESS FOR JOY

Care: He Binghan

EVERYONE HAS THAT one friend who is the comedic relief of the group. For me, that particular person is He Binghan.

He Binghan has the sweetest, most childlike heart of any person I have ever met. He was not the most book-smart kid, as he struggled to read and comprehend what he was reading, but this kid's emotional intelligence was off the charts. He was also incredibly clumsy and aloof, rarely paying attention to what he was doing.

However, when it came to skiing and halfpipe, this kid flat-out knew what he was doing. He knew how to make adjustments, and he made them faster than anyone else. When he skied, he just felt it.

He had an incredible sense of what he was capable of and knew when he was able to push it and when it was not time to push it. We would ask him if he was ready to try a new trick, and he would usually respond, "Tomorrow." But the tricks he did do, once he did them, were some of the biggest and best in the sport.

This kid brought joy everywhere he went. He was always happy. He was always having fun. He was the one to lift everyone's spirits on a bad day.

One day stands out in particular.

We had been training regularly for four months, two hours a day, five days a week in the gym, plus five days a week on snow.

We had just finished the first competition of the season, and our team was tired. They were dragging ass, not wanting to do anything. When they showed up at the gym for a workout, I asked them how they were feeling. (Remember: I don't speak Chinese very well, so these conversations were a bit difficult.)

I asked them how they were feeling:

* thumbs up = Good
* thumbs down = Bad
* thumbs in the middle = So-so.

Everyone gave me a thumbs down.

So, I said, "Okay, what can we do to get you guys to a thumbs up?"

"Sleep," they all said.

I told them that tomorrow was a rest day. "What else could we do to make you feel better?"

"A game!" they said.

"Perfect. Let's play a game."

So, we started our workout by playing a game. It is a version of dodgeball, where we use a large yoga/stability ball to try and tag each other out. We were all having such a good time, playing a game and being kids again, that we forgot we were professional athletes.

That day, we were playing this game out by the pool, because it was right next to the gym where we trained. Ten or so minutes into the game, the ball found its way into the pool. He Binghan went to get the ball out of the pool, but as he touched it, it shot away from him, and he fell into the pool on top of the lane-line buoys.

There he was, halfway into the pool, and everyone stopped dead in their tracks then fell to the ground, laughing. Not just any laugh, but one of those laughs where you start crying and can't stop laughing.

I laughed harder than I had laughed in years.

It was exactly what everyone needed. We were all tired and just wanted or needed to have some fun.

Yes, I train professional athletes, and yes, we play lots of games. Why? Because, when it is your job to train all the time, it gets old. So, you have to find ways to make training fun. If you are not having fun enjoying the process, then you will not enjoy the result.

After we all picked ourselves up off the ground, we had one of our best gym sessions ever. We brought joy back into our training, and that allowed us to enjoy what we did again and make it not a job anymore.

When you enjoy the process, the results do not matter.

Teach: FLOW

Every FLOW activity has something in common: it provides a sense of discovery, a creative feeling of transporting the person doing it to a new reality.

It can push someone to higher levels of performance and lead to previously undreamed-of states of consciousness. It transforms the self by making it more complex. Growth of self is the key to flow activities.

This book, *Cognitive Shift,* is about growing your capacity. Growing your "self" through new experiences. Any activity that transforms the way we see reality is enjoyable. Flow is any activity that provides experiences so gratifying, people are willing to do it for its own sake, with little concern for what they get out of it, even when it is difficult or dangerous to do.

In the beginning, it is highly likely that flow will result from a structured activity or from an individual's ability to make flow occur. Or both! When we first start, we need to learn the rules of flow so we can use our creativity to get into these states in a way that is desirable to us.

Music, skiing, rock climbing, cooking, painting, reading, etc.: what makes these activities flow activities is they are designed to make optimal experience easier to achieve. There are sets of rules to each; they require the learning of skills, the setting of goals, and some essential feedback. These elements make control possible, by facilitating concentration and by making the experience as vivid as possible. They take you out of everyday reality and move you into the reality of the game, creating new experiences with constant variation.

Sports, art, and nature are some examples, because of the ways they are constructed to help participants and spectators attain the experience and achieve an ordered state of mind that is highly enjoyable to them.

The most important components of our experience are *challenge* and *skill*.

We cannot enjoy doing the same thing at the same level for long. We grow bored or frustrated, and the desire to continue to enjoy ourselves pushes us to stretch our skills or discover new opportunities for using our skills.

Research presented the book *The Rise of Superman* by Steven Kotler suggests we need to challenge ourselves by at least four percent greater than our current ability. Any higher and it is too difficult; we get frustrated and stop. Any lower and the activity is not challenging enough; we become bored.

The only rule that matters is that the main reason of doing this activity is to do it for enjoyment.

If you are not enjoying what you are doing, then you will not enjoy the result. Some people argue we need to have discipline. I would argue that the discipline of always doing something you hate creates bad habits and is not sustainable, especially if we plan on enjoying life.

If we want to enjoy our life, we need to find activities that are designed primarily to improve the quality of our experience. The main reason for each activity needs to be enjoyment.

Flow activities are different for everyone. They are freely chosen by each of us and intimately related to what is meaningful to us; which ones we choose to pursue can, in fact, be good indicators of who we are.

Creating opportunities for more flow in our life is a great start. We also need to develop the skills to make use of it. We need to know how to control our consciousness and attention to what we are doing. This is a skill most people have not yet learned to cultivate.

The biggest obstacle for people getting into flow states: our own mind. We are self-conscious about the activities we participate in. We are constantly worried of how others will think and perceive us. We are afraid of not fitting in or failing.

When we have these thoughts going on in the background of our mind, this is an attention disorder. We are not able to focus 100%. In order to get into flow we must be able to have 100% control of our attention. Investing energy into how others perceive us, prevents us from fully engaging and getting to our flow states. It makes it hard to enjoy ourselves, difficult to learn, and forfeit opportunities to grow our capacity.

Train: How do we create more Flow in our lives?

There are two conditions that make flow difficult to experience: lack of rules and ego

Lack of Rules: When it becomes unclear what we can and cannot do, or when we are not clear on what society values, our behavior becomes erratic and meaningless. We have no rules, so we have no idea how to act in society. We do not know what is right. There is no meaning. It is problematic when people depend too much on the rules of society to give order to their lives, because, then if they don't have that, they become anxious.

Ego: Your ego is not your amigo! Our ego leads us to feel that society and the system are going against our beliefs, so we are being judged for what we do and who we are. We have to fit into the system, and we feel alienated, like we do not belong.

When it comes down to it, we cannot get into flow activities if we are anxious or bored. This makes perfect sense, because of what we will learn in coming chapters about our nervous system. It puts us either into survival mode or creation mode.

Survival Mode and Creation Mode

In Survival Mode, we are constantly facing threats and trying to survive. We are anxious. This does not allow us to get into flow states and grow ourselves or our capacity. Instead, we put all of our energy into surviving while in Survival Mode.

When in Creation Mode, we are on the opposite end of the spectrum from where procrastination and boredom live. Boredom also does not allow us to get into flow states in order to grow the self.

We need to find the balance between survival and creation mode, so we continually are able to get into flow states and use those flow states to grow ourselves and our capacity.

Apply: Always be a white belt. Seek variation, seek new experiences, seek cognitive shifts.

Cultivate more flow in your life by creating a process of self-development.

Self-Development = Self-Love.

If we are in survival mode, our attention is only focused on one thing: *surviving*. There is no growth here. We have to stress ourselves to grow, yes, but we cannot enter flow states to grow if we are in survival mode.

We need to get out of survival mode and away from anxiety, so we can find activities that fill us up and allow us to grow our capacity in ways that are enjoyable and meaningful to us.

Here's a recent example of this for me. I bought a skateboard. I was afraid to get on it. My skills were low.

So, I sold my car and forced myself to use my skateboard to get around. Three months later, I still fall every now and again, but the joy it brings me to skate down to the beach every day fills me up with energy and enthusiasm for life. I know how to do it now, and I can keep finding ways to challenge my ability, so I am always continuing to grow my capacity.

For application, get out there and be a white belt again. What is something you have always wanted to try?

From this chapter, we've learned that new experiences are things that help us grow. What are some things out there that have structure and that require us to learn a new skillset and increase our attentional capacity? That is what flow activities are designed to do: teach you how to learn. When you know how to learn, you can decide to develop whatever skills suit you and add meaning to your life.

Most people's problem is they mistake thinking about doing something for actually doing something. But here's the thing: *not* making a decision is a decision.

Confidence is our ability to take action. Get out there and be a white belt again!

Don't say, "I know." When we say "I know," it shuts us off from the opportunity to keep learning and growing.

You will probably fall a few times, like I did on my skateboard, but failure is feedback. If a baby stopped trying to walk every time he or she fell, they would not have survived.

We all have a desire in us. We just need confidence to take action.

CHAPTER 2

LEARNING

Care: Li Songsheng

I HAVE A SPECIAL place in my heart for this guy and this picture is worth the world to me.

These are pictures of Li Songsheng. He was the smallest of the nine athletes on our team. He was the one who spoke the least amount of English and the kid who did not want to listen or do anything. He lived in his own world.

I felt for the little guy. It is tough being in a group of guys who pick on you for being scrawny. I knew that all too well, being the kid with glasses growing up.

I took all of my athletes under my wing. I was not just their coach. At times, I was their big brother, their dad, teacher, coach, and friend.

I wanted to help Songsheng, because he was the weakest. The littlest. I had been there before. Luckily for Songsheng, in me he had a new best friend who was going to show him how to get strong.

Communicating with him was incredibly difficult. For one thing, he really did not want to listen. He knew he was smaller and weaker than the other boys. But I knew that all he needed was someone to believe in him. Someone to give him attention. Someone to play big brother and teach him how to stick up for himself. Someone to show him they cared about him and that he mattered.

First, we had to learn how to communicate. I would hold up my pinky finger to him. I pointed to him and said, "This is you."

I pointed to my thumb and said, "This is me."

I told him he was a skinny pinky. I was a big strong thumb. I let him know my job was going to be to get him to not be a pinky anymore, to become be a big, strong thumb.

How did I do this? I picked on him. The same way an older brother picks on a younger brother. I was not trying to be mean to Songsheng! I just wanted to show him he was just as good as the other boys, if not better. He just had to try. I might have singled him out too much and pushed him harder than I needed to, at times, but that is what's needed, to be great. Someone who believes in you until you begin to believe in yourself.

It turns out strength was not really an issue for Songsheng. He was plenty strong and he moved just as well as the other boys. But he was smaller than the other boys, mainly because he didn't eat enough. He ate like a bird.

So, what did I do? At every meal, as we were finishing up, I would go over and sit with Songsheng. I would look at his plate, then I would look at him with a look on my face that said, "Why have you not finished the food on your plate?"

He would wave a finger, "No, no. Full," and rub his belly.

I did this at every meal. I would encourage him to eat a few more bites. When food came around, I would encourage him to take a few more bites. I would sit next to him and eat with him. When he stopped eating, I would take a bite and let him know it was his turn to take another bite. At times, this was very hard, but he played along like a little brother does. For the first time in a long time, someone clearly cared about him, and someone gave him attention. Someone wanted him to succeed.

This photo of him is from the team's second competition of the season: Junior Worlds in New Zealand. He had started the season as our smallest athlete with the least potential. On that day, though, he surprised everyone. Songsheng sent it. He flew higher than anyone in the competition. And he won First Place.

This had nothing to do with a program or a specific workout. It had everything to do with the fact that someone cared about him. and believed in him. As a result, he learned to believe in himself. Together, we created his process for confidence.

When you have confidence, you can do anything you set your mind to.

Teach: How we learn and unlearn.

Learning = Behavior Change

Our body is designed to handle stress and adapt to it. It remembers stressors so that, next time, it is not such a big deal.

Have you ever thought about that?

How do we develop these reactions to stress? How does our body learn new skills?

In order to learn new skills, we must first learn how the body adapts to stress.

Here is a model for how we learn skills. Our body is designed to be self-sufficient, not self-optimizing. So, it is possible we have learned some bad habits that are harmful to us. Our body doesn't know the difference. Whatever conscious or subconscious energy we put in, our body adapts and strives to be efficient at. This way, it can save brain capacity for higher level more complex functions.

Stages of Learning:

✶ Stage 1: Unconscious Incompetence

"I don't know what I don't know."

✶ Stage 2: Conscious Incompetence

"I know about it, but I am not very good at it."

✶ Stage 3: Conscious Competence

"I know how, but I have to think about it and concentrate on what I have to do."

✶ Stage 4: Unconscious Competence

"I know and I can do it effortlessly."

✶ Stage 5: Flow/Mastery

This is where we want to get. This is what makes life worth living.

This learning process works for all skills. This is our body's neuroplasticity. Whatever task we put conscious energy into, the body strives to remember. It is like walking through a tall, grassy field. The first time it takes a while to find your way carefully through. The second time, we remember, and we can see our path starting to wear down, so it becomes faster. The hundredth time, it is a full-on bike path, paved and so smooth, we can sprint down it as fast as we can without thinking.

We have to take the time and conscious energy to learn and get feedback, before we can make anything subconscious and reach the point where we do not even have to think about it.

When we get to this stage, we have reached mastery and are able to get into these flow states, because we are in control of our conscious and subconscious abilities.

Driving is another good example of this. The first time you do it is scary, and you have to really focus to get your skills up. A few years later, you are eating a cheeseburger, talking on the phone, hitting the kids in the backseat, and telling them to be quiet, all while driving down the road at seventy-five miles per hour.

The human body is really impressive, but only at the stuff we constantly tell it to learn.

What are you telling your body to learn every day? How are you growing your capacity?

Train: Thoughts, Breath, Hydration, Nutrition, Movement, Belonging/Environment, Confidence

This is the structure I look at when deciding what places to attack first with my clients. It goes in order of importance.

1) **Thoughts** = our current reality
2) **Breathe**: if we do not breathe for three minutes, we start to die
3) **Hydration**: if we do not drink water for three days, we die
4) **Nutrition**: if we do not eat for three weeks, we die
5) **Movement**: pressure and tension on the system regulates it
6) **Belonging/Environment:** sense of purpose, and how our environment affects us
7) **Confidence**: the confidence in our capacity to overcome challenges

Where should we focus our attention? Well, it all starts in the mind. We have to have a desire or a need, before we have an action.

The things we think and say are powerful.

Abracadabra—with my words, I create.

We think and speak magic. So, we better spend some time thinking about the thoughts we have. Are our thoughts serving us? What are we focusing on? Where the focus goes, energy flows. No focus, no energy. If it exists in our head, it doesn't exist.

A goal is a dream that is written down. The more you start to think about what it is you want and then write it down and say it over and over again, the more the body can learn how to create it. Not making a decision is a decision, and the body is always listening, trying to make its processes more efficient. If you do nothing, you will get better at doing nothing.

Breathe: our first priority in life is breathing. If we do not breathe for three minutes, our body starts to die.

Most of us have developed less than optimal breathing patterns in our daily lives. We must learn to optimize each breath to maximize our energy. Our breath is our connection to our body. It lets us know we are still alive. It lets us know how the body is experiencing stress.

We must master and optimize this process before moving on to the other processes, or we will have stress-related problems and not be able to live to maximize our capacity.

Breathe More. Feel Better.

Hydration: If we do not drink water for three days, we die. Even before then, if we are not properly hydrated, our body suffers, performance-wise. We have a drop in our cognition and accumulate brain fog. Dehydration stresses the body and puts us in survival mode.

We cannot get into flow states or live our best life in survival mode. We must learn how to optimize our hydration so our health and performance are maximizing our capacity.

Nutrition: If we do not eat for three weeks, our body will break itself down and cease to function. We need to find the appropriate way to fuel or body.

Everybody is different and has had different experiences, so our fuel sources will vary. We need to figure out what types of fuel are optimal for us.

We also need to look at the process of digestion. What foods are hard for our body to process? What foods fuel us up with energy, and what foods slow us down?

We want to spend the minimum effective dose on nutrition, so no wasted energy is put towards digestion that could otherwise be used to grow our capacity.

Movement: We need to move every day. Movement brings balance and homeostasis to the body. Once we start resting instead of moving and doing, we start dying. We are either growing or dying. That is why it says "rest in peace" on your gravestone. You stopped growing your capacity.

Again, we need to strive for the minimum effective dose. Too much movement and we have to spend too much energy to recover. Not enough and we are not stressing the body appropriately, which leads to depression and anxiety.

Environment/Belonging: Humans are social creatures. We need others to make us feel like we belong. The environments we are in have a huge impact on everything going on. We must look at our environments to find out if they are serving us. Are they helping us to grow our capacity? Or, in this environment, am I in survival mode?

The last part is confidence, which is what this book is about. We need confidence in our abilities so we can continue to grow our capacity.

In order to have confidence, we need to celebrate wins. Wins can be anything. A win is anything you did to grow your capacity. It could be as small as reading this book or waking up today. Celebrating wins, builds momentum.

Momentum builds confidence, and confidence allows to build capacity to do more things.

Apply: Learning or Unlearning?

We stay young when we keep learning. You can teach an old dog new tricks. Neuroplasticity works that way. The things we focus on constantly leads those pathways to become stronger and stronger. The things we stop focusing on leads those pathways to begin to fade away, leaving them available for us to create new pathways.

As long as we keep learning, we will keep growing our capacity. The body needs pressure and tension for it to keep growing. As long as we keep applying that pressure and tension, the body will continue to respond.

The beauty about it is we get to choose what things we want to learn and how we want to grow our capacity. That is what makes life exciting: we get to create whatever we want. We just have to learn how to learn or, more importantly, how to unlearn our bad habits and any our old ways of thinking that have held us back.

Our beliefs can be hardwired into us and prevent us from becoming the person we dream of, but that is where new experiences and cognitive shifts are required. We need new experiences and stimulation to constantly challenge our beliefs, so we can change our behavior to match that of what we desire more.

People don't change unless they change their mind.

CHAPTER 3

ADAPTATION

Care: Zhang Kexin

THIS GIRL, ZHANG KEXIN, is one of the fiercest competitors I have ever met. In her sport, she is in the top three in the world. She has won many events and, at the last Olympics, was a ninth-place finisher. In 2022, there is no doubt in my mind she will be on that podium.

The craziest thing about Zhang Kexin is she is not very talented. Zhang Kexin is like me, which is probably why I like her. She is a strong human being. She should have been a weightlifter. And she is not just physically strong. This girl is the most mentally tough person I have probably ever met. To be perfectly honest, she terrifies me.

This picture tells an incredible story about her. Here in this picture, you can see she is pissed off and frustrated, separating herself from the rest of the group. Why? Because she was not as talented as the other girls on the trampoline.

Kexin was better in the halfpipe than the other girls, but when it came to the trampoline and flipping and spinning, she was by far the worst. This was no fault of her own: the other girls all had a gymnastics background and many more years of experience. But that didn't matter to her. She wanted to be the best. When she was not the best at something, she got pissed.

We struggled in the beginning, because we had to take her back to the basics. We had to get her to remove her bad habits. She was the best athlete on the team. She wanted to spend no time on the boring basics. So she had to unlearn her bad habits in order to learn higher level tricks.

In the weight room, I kid you not, this girl should have gone to the summer Olympics for weightlifting. She was so strong, so explosive, so flexible, and so damned stubborn that anything you told her to do, she would do. When it came to skiing, flipping, and spinning, though, she needed help.

So, what did we do? We celebrated the wins in the weight room. She outworked everyone. Out of all nine athletes, I never had to worry about her working hard enough. She wanted to be the best so badly. So much so that it frustrated and angered her when the other girls were better than her. She would get so mad and frustrated, she almost fought one of the Chinese staff members for helping one of the other athletes before her. She had a fiery passion. We just had to channel that passion for good.

Our first month and a half together, I couldn't tell if she hated me or that's just how she was. She was the leader of the team, but she was behaving horribly because she was struggling.

This all changed when we got to China for the first time. During our first workout in the gym in China, it was 92 degrees and so humid, you would sweat walking outside.

It was a horrible workout. The athletes were giving zero effort. Except for Kexin. She always worked hard in the gym, no matter what. She was the only one working out and putting in effort that first day in China. Afterward, I sent her a message. I told her I was proud of her for always putting forth her best effort, even when it was not ideal or when your teammates were slacking off. I told her she was a great role model for this team and a leader, and her hard work would soon pay off.

She thanked me and told me the only reason she worked so hard was because her family was poor. She was only skiing to send money back, so her family could have a better life. This sixteen-year-old girl, who was one of the best in the world, was competing in a sport only to support her family. I told her she was an incredible inspiration to me as well as to the rest of this team.

Over the next few weeks, she changed. She became the team leader I knew she would be. She worked harder. She pushed the other girls and athletes to do the same. She knew, if she was going to get back to the Olympics and the podium, she needed a team who was going to push her to be her best every day. She already knew she was on track, now that she had me, but she also pushed the rest of the team to step it up.

Fast forward to four months later, at the second world cup event of the year in China. Kexin showed up and was the champion everyone knew she could be. She won the world cup event in China. Here is was a picture of her just after that event. This girl had found her confidence, and it was not going away anytime soon.

A few months later, at the world championships, she ended up in third place. She went from ninth place to third place in one season. She is still not the most talented girl out there, but you can never count this girl out, because she is a competitor, and she wants it more than you do. She is stronger than you mentally and physically and is willing to take a beating, only to get up and do it again.

This picture of her winning the event in China clearly shows that she was confident and she was going to be a champion not matter what anyone said.

Teach: Adaptation: Our Nervous System

"Man should not try to avoid stress any more than he would shun food, love or exercise."

"Adopting the right attitude can convert a negative stress into a positive one."

Hans Seyle is an endocrinologist who conducted important scientific research on the stress response of an organism to stressors. He was one of the first men to demonstrate the existence of biological stress, and actually coined the term "stress." (I define stress in the way the body senses it: pressure and tension.)

Seyle conceptualized stress into having two components: a set of responses (known as the General Adaptation Syndrome) and the development of a pathological state from ongoing unrelieved stress.

The General Adaptation Syndrome is a three-stage process that describes the physiological changes the body goes through when under stress.

Stage 1: Alarm Reaction Stage

The alarm reaction stage refers to the initial symptoms the body experiences when under stress. This is known as the Flight or Freeze response. (Fight is a trained response; more on that later.) This natural reaction prepares you to either flee or protect yourself in dangerous situations.

Stage 2: Resistance Stage

After the initial shock of a stressful event and after having a flight or freeze response, the body begins to repair itself. If you overcome the stress and the situation is no longer an issue, your body continues to repair itself to its pre-stress state.

If the stress continues for extended periods of time, your body remains on high alert. Your body eventually adapts and learns how to live at a higher stress level. In this stage the body goes through changes in an attempt to cope with stress.

If the resistance stage continues for too long without a pause to offset the effects of stress, this leads to the exhaustion stage.

Signs of resistance stage include:

- ✓ Irritability
- ✓ Frustration
- ✓ Poor Concentration

Stage 3: Exhaustion Stage

This stage is a result of prolonged chronic stress. Stress for long periods of time can drain your physical, emotional, and mental resources to a point where the body no longer has the capacity to manage stress.

Signs of exhaustion include:

- ✓ Fatigue
- ✓ Burn-out
- ✓ Depression
- ✓ Anxiety
- ✓ Decreased adaptability

The physical effects of this stage weaken your immune system and put you at risk for stress-related illnesses. This can happen with any type of stress. The body does not know the difference between types of stress. We want to be efficient and use the minimum effective dose.

The exhaustion stage is also known as overtraining. I once set out to prove that overtraining was a myth. I believed that the body could take any stresses we place on it, as long as we got appropriate recovery. There is no such thing as overtraining, only under-recovering.

I do still believe this to be true. However, what I learned is that the body does not just take into account your training stress. It takes into account all of your life stress—emotional, spiritual, and relationships. Stress is stress, and if you have a life stress going on, your body has to spend conscious energy thinking about it, which makes it harder for you to get into those flow states and achieve growth. We want to *minimize* our conscious effort to deal with stress so we can *maximize* growing our capacity.

How our Nervous System works: Survival mode & Creation mode.

Breathing is life. Breathing is creating. Stop breathing, stop creating.

Breathing is both a conscious and a subconscious process. The more we are able to access our subconscious and listen to what it is telling us, the better decisions we will make and, ultimately, the better we will be able to adapt.

Making the subconscious conscious: your body is self-regulating not self-optimizing. If this were not true, then we would not need to train at all. Just because we are not aware of our breathing doesn't mean we are doing it right.

Subconscious behaviors are behaviors we are not really aware of. We want to use our breath to connect to our subconscious. It makes us more aware of our behaviors. When we are more aware of our behaviors, we can make better decisions. Our breath allows us to be more aware of what is going on throughout the day, and if we are more aware, we are able to make better decisions.

Our breath connects us to our nervous system.

Our nervous system:

Sympathetic overview: "Flight" or "Freeze." "Fight" is a trained response, or an adaptation.

➢ Responsible for ensuring survival. "STRESS" = "SURVIVAL MODE"
➢ Our physiology drives us towards action:
   • Increased heart rate
   • Increased respiration, decrease in CO_2 alters chemistry and affects our ability to deal with stress long-term

- Release neurotransmitters to recruit more muscle fibers
- ➢ Decrease blood flow to organs
  - Dilates pupils to narrow field of vision and increase focus
  - Tend to lose fine motor skills and rely on gross motor patterns, unless we have trained something specifically our body defaults to very few options around: protecting vital organs, help us flee danger.

If we are sympathetic too long, we start to experience is anxiety. Anxiety is a sympathetic response to a new threatening event. Our brain is predicting stress, so it increases sympathetic. This can cause unnecessary tension. Can cause you to lose sleep or lead to decreased quality of sleep. This is where we make poor decisions.

Parasympathetic Overview: Rest, Digest and Recovery, or Feed and Breed. "CREATION MODE"

➢ Anabolic in nature

> ➤ Rebuilding tissues (not just from exercise but general wear and tear)
> ➤ Increase blood flow to organ systems
> ➤ Helps optimize healing process so we can continue to experience new stressors.
> ➤ Most calm and clear thinking, problem solving and creativity.

When the actions of parasympathetic nervous system are balanced well with sympathetic, we are optimized and functioning properly and generally very productive.

Parasympathetic is anabolic in nature and is classically organized as rest, digest, and recover. As a result, we find that, when we are in this system, we have increased blood flow to the organs, which allow sour physiology maximum optimization. This in turn is what allows us, as a species, to deal with and handle new and novel stimuli.

We are not great at transitioning between states.

Animals, when threatened, get highly sympathetic. Like both the lion and the gazelle, when being chased or hunting, regardless of the outcome. For the lion, it rests to return to a parasympathetic place by taking a nap. If the gazelle escapes, it goes back to grazing for rest and digest.

As humans, we have our modern-day stressors, but then, instead of going to a parasympathetic place, we have to go talk about it with others or put it on social media, and we never get to the parasympathetic. The balance of our sympathetic and parasympathetic states affects our ability to adapt to our environment.

The balance between the two systems:

➢ Living in sympathetic leads to anxiety and stress.
➢ Living in parasympathetic leads to depression and procrastination.

We want to be able to switch between the two, to be the most adaptable human.

Our behaviors go back and forth between the two based off of our environment.

Now we know about how our body adapts and how that is controlled by the input received by the nervous system, which then makes the best decisions and action. If we are stressed, we are less likely to make a good decision. Learning to balance our systems is key, if we want to adapt and grow our capacity to be who it is we desire to be.

Now, how can we train our nervous system?

Train: Training our nervous system. Adaptability

Our adaptability is our ability to adapt to a stressor. The quicker we are able to adapt after a stress, the more adaptable we are and the more we are able to grow our capacity. So, how do we train our adaptability?

First, we must understand the signs our body is sending us. Our body was perfectly designed to deal with stress and to grow. We intuitively know what we need, but we have lost the ability to hear the signs it is giving us.

The best measure of adaptability is heart rate and HRV. Our heart rate is a direct reflection of the stress in our lives. For example, when we start running, that is a stress. In order to match the stress, our heart rate increases to meet the demand.

An increased heart rate then tells us we are experiencing stress.

As a coach, I would look at an athlete's resting heart rate in the morning. I am not looking at any particular range of numbers; I am looking for patterns. If an athlete's resting heart rate in the morning is regularly 50-55 bpm and then, one day, increases to 70bpm, I might have concern. This athlete's heart is working harder than normal. That must mean they are stressed out about something and not recovering or not adapting. It is a sign we could be headed into the exhaustion stage.

It is okay to have a higher resting HR, especially if you are training hard, but we want to make sure this does not become a chronic issue leading to exhaustion and overtraining. These are signs of our tensions and pressures.

Tension and pressure are how we learn to adapt. To create. To explore.

It is intuitive. We have forgotten how to listen to the "tensions" and "pressures" on our body. We, instead, rely on technology and AI to use algorithms for heart rate HRV and sleep. While we humans are the most technologically advanced piece of technology that exists, we have not yet learned how to listen to it.

We have stopped listening to it and stopped trusting it. We slam our body with stress and hope it adapts and doesn't break. Or we never stress ourselves enough and are docile and complacent.

The best way to understand how we learn to adapt is to watch babies learn to move. In order for a baby to first learn to move, it must have a desire. It must have a reason or a want to move. With no desire comes no action. That desire leads to action.

When we are a baby, we have no idea or awareness of our body. We just start moving, and our nervous system receives feedback from our internal and external environments. From that feedback, we gain knowledge.

For example, we have to experience hunger. In order to get our needs met, we have to ingest food. We are not quite capable of doing this on our own yet. So, we cry. We take action. From that action, our mom hears us and feeds us. As a baby, we now remember this experience, so, when it happens again, we know how to create the action that creates the result we desire.

The same thing happens when we first begin to walk. We have a desire to go somewhere. In order to first start moving, we have to apply pressure and tension to our muscles and then press into the ground to create movement. We move our arms and legs in an attempt to move. We then get feedback of results. Did we get where we wanted to go? No. Okay, keep trying. Babies are consumed by curiosity and the desire to have new experiences. They do not let failure stop them from what they want.

We have lost this childlike curiosity.

For the first few years of their lives, babies are always stressing themselves out and constantly learning new skills, wiring their nervous system to memorize these basic functions. Babies are not exempt from the GAS theory.

That is why babies sleep so much. They spend so much energy learning new skills, they need to shut down all the time and sleep to recover. If they do not shut down and recover, they can enter the stages of resistance, as well. We have all seen this in babies, when they get tired and cranky. They cannot control their emotions, and they get frustrated with little things. Adults do the same thing when they are stressed. We get cranky and make poor decisions when we should probably take a nap.

The second thing I like looking at with myself and athletes is HRV. Now, it is getting easier to measure this with technology. It is still not the most accurate, but again, we are just looking for patterns.

HRV stands for heart rate variability. Beats per minute means how many times the heart beats in a minute. Heart Rate Variability is the difference in the time between beats. We want more variability in the time between. More variability means our body is more adaptable. Less variability indicates our body is stressed and less likely to adapt to new stresses.

Many people will argue about the validity to current technology, but having something reliable and consistent, so you can see significant change, is what you are looking for.

I have tracked my Resting Heart Rate and HRV, for me as well as for my athletes. Having the insight into how they are adapting and recovering gives me some information, so I can ask some better questions about how they are recovering. Then, we can implement a strategy.

I have also found that you do not need fancy devices or equipment to do this. Our body, again, is very intuitive, and we know when we are stressed-out. We just have to look for the signs.

One test I have found to be a good indicator of the body's adaptability and readiness to take on stress is the CO-2 test.

As we learned, breathing is both a conscious and a subconscious pattern. As we breathe, we take in oxygen and get rid of CO-2. If we hold our breath, CO-2 builds up in our bloodstream and causes the blood to get more acidic, causing the body to trigger your brain to want to breathe.

If we are in a relaxed state and not stressed out, we are able to better manage this CO-2 level and know we have plenty of air. However, if our body is recovering from stress and we hold our breath, we do not have as much capacity to deal with this stress as it rises in our body, so we cannot hold our breath as long.

This CO-2 test is a great way to test your body's readiness to take on stress.

Apply: The CO-2 Test and Down-Regulating activities.

CO_2 tolerance test gauges our personal ability to deal with stress.

Our ability to deal with CO_2 (waste) in the body can give us a good indication about our physiological state. I have found it to be a good indicator of a person's emotional reactivity, but also their ability to deal with stress.

I highly suggest everyone use this test every day, in the morning. This will assess your body's ability to deal with stress. Are we recovered from the day before? I also suggest finding a way to track your resting heart rate in the morning.

This test, if done consistently, will show you your ability to breathe can be improved. It will give you good insight each day by checking in with your body to see how it is adapting.

To do this test, sit or lie in a comfortable position—it does not matter which. What does matter, however, is that you do this test and then repeat it the same way every time, for consistency.

Take three breaths in the nose and out the mouth. On the fourth breath, inhale and, as soon as you start exhaling, start a stopwatch. Try to exhale as slowly as you can. As soon as you stop exhaling, stop the timer.

If you would like to see a video explanation of this test please go to:

http://optimizedlifestylecoaching.com/co2-test/

CO_2 tolerance scores:

- <0:20   High stress
- 0:20-0:40 Normal
- 0:40-1:00 Good
- >1:00 Very Good
- >1:20 Excellent

The first time I did this test, I was 0:14. I panicked. That is okay. This is the first time you are doing the test. Learning how to breathe with better mechanics will improve your ability to take in oxygen. As time goes on, you will also get better at being able to slow your exhale down.

When you first start out, it is very stressful to do this, and you feel panicked. That is normal. That is your body having to deal with the increased amount of CO_2 in your blood. This make your blood more acidic, so your body sends warning signals that CO_2 is building and you need to breathe.

However, you have enough oxygen to last. But when our nervous system is stressed, we have less control over our ability to deal with stress. This is why this is a good test to do each day, to see how ready your body is to deal with stress.

Keep a log. You will find that you get better quickly. I started at :14 seconds. A week later, I was at :40 seconds. I find myself usually around :40-:50 seconds. This is my baseline. If I have a day where I wake up and am only able to get :30 seconds, I know that, hey, my body is stressed. Maybe I will take it easier today or focus on recovering my body, so it can better adapt to the stresses on it. I also have had days where I have hit 1:15 as my best. On those days, I know my body is really primed and ready to take on any stresses life throws at me.

Our body was intelligently designed so we can adapt to the stresses of our environment. However, in order to adapt, we must give the body the appropriate resources to recover. It is also important to note, if we do not stress ourselves, we do not adapt. This leads to procrastination.

Apply: Creating a breathwork practice; up-regulate and down-regulate

Breathing has the ability to regulate cortisol/adrenaline levels.

Upregulation: a physical state associated with stress and survival that manifests itself as tension, clenching, and rigidity in the body, breath, and mind.

- Fast breath, shallow breath, increased cortisol production.
- Increased adrenaline production, narrowing of vision.
- Enhanced survival mode, tension throughout the body.

> ➤ Clenching of the jaw or facial muscles, bracing for impact

Downregulation: a physical state associated with relaxation and growth that manifests itself as calmness, deliberate movement and flexibility in the body, breath, and the mind.

> ➤ Smooth breath, deep breath
> ➤ Decrease in cortisol and adrenaline, field of vision increases.
> ➤ Increase in growth hormone production, general relaxation.
> ➤ Greater access to flow states and improved pelvic floor health

We live in a perpetually upregulated or stressed-out culture. It is up to us to be an expert in our own physiology. We need to develop a breathwork practice through which we can get good at relaxation and downregulation, in order to have a shot a balance, calmness, and peace.

Our society glorifies up-regulation. Down-regulation is for the weak. We have a work hard/play harder mentality. We are addicted to up-regulation.

Down-regulation activities:

➢ Walking, deep breathing, smiling, yin yoga
➢ -Soft tissue work (massage), sensory deprivation tanks
➢ -Meditation, unstructured play (flow states)
➢ -Down-regulating music, dancing

Up-regulating has its place. We need to find activities that allow us to down-regulate and exit the stressed-out mode. If we want to adapt to stress, we need to have activities that take us down and let us get to that parasympathetic state.

Developing a breathwork practice or a practice of self-love is the best way to do this.

This is a process, and you should try many things to find out what works for you. Developing a consistent practice of self-love and gratitude is a great way for the body to handle and recover from stress. We will learn in the next section how to cultivate more energy, and we will find that down-regulating and up-regulating activities allow us to control our energy and focus and attention throughout the day.

Ultimately, developing a self-love practice is great at helping us deal with stress and how to better adapt. But what we really need to be paying attention to is *sleep*. Sleep is the only way we truly recover from stress. If we have stress, our quality of sleep suffers. If the quality of our sleep suffers, our energy and adaptations suffer.

In the next chapter, we will learn how to cultivate and manage our energy, so we are able to adapt to life's stresses and so we are sleeping and recovering appropriately in order to continue to grow our capacity.

CHAPTER 4

ENERGY

Care: Wu Meng

THERE ARE PEOPLE in this world who, when they do things, seem to do them effortlessly and perfectly, no matter what. That is Wu Meng.

What amazed me about this girl is that she never looks as if she is trying. If it was skiing or in the weight room, she always was putting in the least amount of effort. However, when she was moving, she moved effortlessly, flawlessly.

She was not one of the athletes in the group whom you could push. She was a typical fourteen-year-old female, more concerned with boys and looking pretty. If you pushed her, that's when her fourteen-year-old-girl attitude came out. If you pushed, she tried less.

She was not willing to be uncomfortable. This held her back. She was an incredibly gifted gymnast and moved better than anyone on the team, but when it came time to learn new tricks, she was not willing to try. Because she always did everything perfectly, she was not willing to try something, if it was not going to be perfect. It crippled her progress.

I always knew when she was up to learning a trick or something new, because as she would go flying through the air, and you could hear her make noises and yell and squeal. She was afraid to try new things, because she didn't want to fail. When she wanted to, though, she could do anything she chose. But only when she wanted to.

Then one day, something happened. We were out at the halfpipe in China, at practice. Our best girl,

Kexin, was not skiing, because she was dealing with some hamstring issues. The leader was out, and the rest of the team seemed to be checked-out, as they were skiing poorly.

Out of nowhere, Wu Meng had a lights-out day. All of a sudden, she was the star of the show. She hit a 900 for the first time, and it was one of the prettiest things I have ever seen. When she landed, she let out a typical Wu Meng squeal, like she always did. But this one was different: this was a confident, proud squeal. The moment was hers, and she shined the brightest that day.

Yes, it took her longer to get there, but the result was so beautiful.

Wu Meng is a perfect example of what you can do when you only use the minimum effective dose. She only did the least amount needed to get by. She knew her body better than anyone, and she knew when and how hard she could push herself.

Because she only ever did the minimum effective dose and moved flawlessly, this girl was never hurt. She never missed a practice due to injury.

People like Wu Meng might take a long time to see progress, but consistency beats intensity all of the time. This girl was exactly that consistent. She just needed the right opportunity to shine.

Great performances are not lucky. They occur when great preparation meets the right opportunity. When she had the opportunity, she capitalized. Hitting that 900 gave her the confidence, so, a few months later, she saw even more progress and hit a 1080.

Teach: Creating our own energy formula.

The more you lose yourself in something bigger than yourself, the more energy you will have.

Insanity is doing the same thing over and expecting a different result.

"We cannot solve our problems with the same thinking we used when we created them."

Everything that exists in your life does so because of two things: something you did or something you didn't do.

I bring up Einstein because, if we are going to talk energy formulas, there is no better person to listen to than the man who created the energy formula himself.

Einstein found out that energy and mass are linked together by a constant, the speed of light. Our mass is determined by this constant, the speed of light. I believe our mass is created by a constant, too: our thoughts. What we constantly think about. Not just consciously but subconsciously. Where the focus goes, the energy flows.

If our mass is equal to our energy, then Einstein equated that 1 kilogram of mass is equivalent to the same amount of energy in 795 million gallons of gasoline. The potential energy of the body is enormous. How can we learn to create our own energy formula, to maximize the amount of energy each of us has on a daily basis?

Imagine what we can accomplish with access to all of that energy! The problem is, however, we are focusing on the wrong things. We need to shift our focus to our attention. Where are we putting all of our attention on a daily basis? Is it serving us? Are the things we are doing filling us up with energy? Or draining us of energy?

Are we sleeping enough, so we are recovering from stress?

Energy, stress, and adaptation are just parts of an equation. We need to balance our formula. If we are spending more energy than we have, we are breaking ourselves down. If we are generating more energy than we need, we have the ability to use that energy to create whatever we desire.

In order to do this, we must first learn to fill up our cup first. We must take care of ourselves first. If we are not full of energy, how can others expect us to fill them up? We cannot fill from an empty cup. We must learn to fill our cup, so we can fill others' from an overflowing cup.

This must be done through a delicate balance of cultivating our own energy. First, we must take a look at where we are spending our energy and determine whether it is the most effective and efficient place to be spending out energy. Once we begin to manage our energy, we can learn how to structure our schedule and our lives to maximize the amount of energy we get from our days. The more energy we cultivate, the greater the potential to grow our capacity and continue to grow it!

Train: The minimum effective dose.

In order to maximize our effectiveness and efficiency with our energy, we must learn the skill of the minimum effective dose required to change.

What is the least amount of energy or effort or stress required to force my body to adapt? We want to find this point. We want to find it because, if we put more energy into working harder than the body needs to adapt, we have to spend more energy on the other side to recover. If we use the minimum amount of energy to stress the body, the minimum amount to cause adaptation, we do not need to use more energy to recover. When we use the minimum effective dose, we save more energy for other processes, allowing us to do more with less.

This is a huge problem for us as a society. We think the "more is better" approach is the way to go. We take the bodybuilder approach, thinking, if one pill gets us this result, then four pills will get us four times the results.

More is not better. Better is better.

The body needs time to adapt and grow capacity. If we push it too far too fast, it breaks, and we have to spend more time to get it back to where it was. It is dancing the fine line of how much is too much and how much is not enough. We are striving to be just right all the time.

We see examples of this get exaggerated with sleep. The only way our body truly recovers from stress and adapts is through sleep. However, instead of taking the bodybuilder approach and saying eight hours of sleep is the minimum effective dose, we think that spending more time awake doing things will allow us to get more done. Again, more is not better. Better is better.

So, we cut ourselves short on sleep. We wear the lack of sleep like a badge of honor. Why get eight hours of sleep when I can get four hours of sleep and get much more done?

This is our thinking when it comes to sleep. Chronic stress is responsible for chronic disease. Stress is not letting us sleep. Not sleeping and recovering is having a long-term huge impact on our health. We are chronically stressed out and energy-depleted.

We need to find a way to cultivate more energy, so we can manage our stress more effectively, so we can sleep, so we can continue to adapt and grow our capacity.

Apply: Energy Cultivation/Management

Notice how I said "energy cultivation and management," not "time cultivation and management." Everyone seems to think they need more time to get things done, when, in fact, everyone has the same amount of time. It is our energy and focus and the intensity of the energy and focus of our attention that really gets things done.

How can we manage our schedule to create more time and energy to get everything done?

Well, for me, I sit down for an hour each week and plan and schedule my week out.

An hour might sound like lots of time to spend on scheduling, but by doing this, I know exactly where all of my energy and attention is going.

When I start my scheduling, I schedule myself first. This is where most people struggle. Sure, we all have responsibilities and people who need our attention. However, if you want to have more energy to invest into growing your capacity, you need to find time to invest in yourself.

Where are you taking time off to recover?

When are you scheduling time for your self-care, your breathwork practice, your movement practice, reading, and education?

If we are to keep growing our capacity, we need to start by scheduling ourselves first. We must fill our own cup up first, if we are to help others. Just like how, on an airplane in an emergency, you put on your own mask on first and save your own life before helping to take care of anyone else.

We all need to learn a little more personal responsibility and put ourselves first, not put our health and wellness in someone else's hands. It is up to us to create our health, wealth, and happiness. So, spending an hour a week on scheduling our time and energy is incredibly important. It helps us find out where our energy is going.

When scheduling yourself, first make sure to schedule:

- ✓ Time off, self-care, workouts, education, and reading
- ✓ Hobbies, adventures, and vacations
- ✓ New experiences/flow activities (always be a white belt)

Take control of your time.

We also want to look at things like our bank account and our schedule. These two places give us good insight into where we are spending our time and energy and what we value.

Look at your schedule. Where do you spend most of your time? Is it at work? Is it commuting? Are you scheduling time for your workouts? Is there time for growing your capacity? Where is all of your time and energy going? Are you aware of it?

Another great place to look, in order to get insight into where you're investing all of your time and attention, is your bank account. Money is also energy. Where are you spending it? Are you spending it at the bar? Are you spending it on food? What things are you valuing?

Taking a look at our bank statement and our schedule gives us good insight into where we are investing our attention. In order to keep growing our capacity, we must find more ways to cultivate more energy to invest in ourselves.

Find more time to invest your energy and attention into yourself. We have the highest ROI when it comes to investing our time.

Other things we need to consider, when looking at where our energy or attention is going, is Environment. Is our environment supportive of what we are trying to do? Are the people in my environment filling me up with energy or draining me? Are the people in my environment inspiring me to be my best self? Or are they distracting my energy from where it needs to go?

This can be hard for people to understand. Our friends might not actually be our friends. They could be distracting us or holding us back, by having us place our energy in places that are not serving us. Or we all have the one friend whom we love them to death but, after interacting with them, we feel drained and tired.

We need to look at our environments and our relationships as energy transactions. Is this relationship or environment filling me up or draining me?

Once we have a good idea of what sort of activities and people fill us up, we can craft our schedule with things that fill us up with energy, followed by something that drains us. That way, we are constantly spending energy and recovering energy, so we are constantly adapting and adding to our capacity.

It gets hard because, in order to get better at this, we must get better at saying no. We have to develop boundaries for our friends and family. We must know what things to say yes to that will help us grow and what to say no to that will stress us out.

Learning to say no to other people is incredibly difficult. We want to make everyone feel happy and accepted. However, saying yes to someone else is saying no to ourselves. The more we say no to ourself, the more energy we give away to other people. The more energy we give away to other people, the less we have to deal with our own stress and thus our capacity for growth.

I am not saying you have to say no to everyone all the time, but learning to be more selfish with your time and energy is the only way we can truly begin to have more energy to create more capacity for ourselves. The more capacity we have, the better we are able to help others. We cannot help others if we are unable to help ourselves first.

Be selfish with your time and energy.

In order to make this change, we must become more aware of our own energy levels. When we are working and begin to feel tired, we need to start noticing this. We need to notice when it is time to stop. When we feel we are no longer sharp, stop and take a break.

It is okay when we run out of energy. Our body has many systems within it to create more energy. They just take time to get going. Think of when you first started running. It feels really awful and hard to breathe. But a few minutes in, your oxidative system kicks in and starts using oxygen to produce more energy. But it takes a second.

If we push past our energy reserves, we enter survival mode. Survival mode is where we make poor decisions. Our poor decisions then take more energy to recover from than had we just stopped for a minute and recovered our energy.

We want to make sure we are effective with our energy. Effectiveness is doing the right thing. Once we are sure we are doing the right thing, then we can strive for more efficiency. Efficiency is doing the thing right. We do not want to do the wrong thing efficiently, though—that is no good.

When it comes to programming our time and energy, just like programing a workout, it is not necessarily about adding more. It is about what can we take out that makes everything easier?

Keep it simple. The simple things require the least amount of energy and still get the adaptation we are looking for. It is as simple as sitting down and looking at your schedule to see where your attention and energy is going.

What we measure, we manage. Everyone can use more energy to get things done.

CHAPTER 5

MOTIVATION

Care: Li Fanghui

THIS IS THE ATHLETE all coaches dream of having. The athlete who will do whatever you say, because they want to be the best. We would tell Fanghui to do ten, and she would do twelve. She wanted to be the best. This, unfortunately, was not always the case. In order to have this desire to be great, we must have our most basic human needs met.

When I first met Li Fanghui, she could not walk without being in pain. Six months prior, she'd injured her knee. She was crying and wincing in pain when she moved. We were told she was the best skier on the team by far, but she was not recovering from her injury.

She was in a lot of pain and not getting the help she needed. The Chinese medical staff was doing the best they could, but they were not able to get her out of pain.

The good news for her was that she was now in my care, along with the care of our Western athletic trainer, my good friend Misao. When it comes to injuries, I rely on having a great team around me to let me know the best way to help our athletes get back from an injury.

Misao and I evaluated Fanghui and told her yes, we could help her. It was not going to be easy, but we would get her skiing again. This girl lit up like a Christmas tree. She had been in pain for months with no relief, so to finally hear we were going to get her better—she was all in. She had people who were supporting her.

Misao took care of getting rid of inflammation and pain in two weeks, while I focused my attention on making this girl as strong as she could be, so she could ski again with the team.

It started out slowly. We collected wins each day. Each day, we got her less pain and more range of motion. We kept her training with the team, so she felt like she was still included. Each day, there was a new win. While she was not able to start skiing with the team, she was able to start bouncing on the trampoline again. She worked with me doing exercises to increase her strength, so she could handle the forces of skiing.

When we got to China, we were training on the water ramps. Her knee was strong enough to handle the water ramps. She was so excited to put her ski boots back on again and be able to do everything with the team.

A month later, we arrived in New Zealand for halfpipe training. By then, she was strong enough to start skiing again. We took it slow and held her back as long as we could. This was her first time back on snow, and she was so excited to be skiing again. It is what she loved to do.

It took a few more months for her to get back into skiing shape and doing tricks in the halfpipe. We clearly started to see that everyone was right: she was by far the best skier on the team.

You cannot be the best version of yourself if you are not taking care of the basic human needs. The body needs to heal. It also needs a social support system to feel safe. Once Li Fanghui got the support she needed and took care of her basic human needs, she was back to being the best version of herself.

In eight months, she went from not being able to walk without pain to being the fifth-best girl in the world in ski halfpipe.

Teach: Abraham Maslow

Abraham Maslow was an American psychologist best known for creating Maslow's hierarchy of needs, a theory of psychological health predicated on fulfilling innate human needs in priority, culminating in self-actualization.

"What a man can be, he must be. This need we call self-actualization."

"What is necessary for a person to change is for a person to change his awareness of himself."

"If you plan on being anything less than you are capable of being, you will probably be unhappy all the days of your life."

"The story of the human race is the story of men and women selling themselves short."

"One can choose to go back toward safety or forward, toward growth. Growth must be chosen again and again; fear must be overcome again and again."

This is the theory of motivation. In order to be the person we know we can be, we must first have our most basic human needs met. We cannot do anything great if we are not adapting to stress.

As we learned in previous chapters, in order for us to get into flow states and grow our capacity and potential as a human being, we must be in creation mode. We must not have stresses that take away our attention from these flow activities.

This is a huge problem in our society. Modern-day society, technology, and convenience have made it so that we are maladapted to be in this environment. 75% of us are obese or overweight. That means 75% of us are not getting our most basic needs met. We are chronically stressed out, or we are not causing enough stress for our bodies to adapt.

When we are not able to have flow in our lives, we are not growing. When we are not growing, we are going the other way and dying. Not stressing ourselves enough leads to procrastination, a low sense of self-worth and belonging, and also depression, which then causes anxiety.

80% of chronic disease is preventable through lifestyle changes. Lifestyle changes need to be based around meeting our most basic human needs.

So, as we have learned in this book so far, the most important thing we need is sleep. If we are not sleeping, we are not recovering from stress. If we have unmanaged stress, we will not be able to the pyramid, below, until we have met our most basic needs.

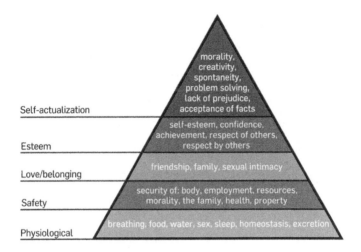

So, in order to be who we know we can be, we must meet our basic needs first. Once we meet our basic needs, we can then start investing more energy into our desires.

How do we go about meeting our most basic human needs?

We set goals. What is the most important thing that needs to happen next?

Make a goal about it.

Not just any goal. We need to create *powerful* goals.

In order to reach our goals, we must have more energy. If we are not meeting our most basic human needs, then we are not cultivating enough energy to adapt to stress. We now know how to cultivate more energy, but what is it we want to invest our energy into? Who is it we want to become?

Train: Goal-Setting—setting powerful goals and being unreasonable with your life.

It is okay if you do not know who you want to be or what you want to do with your life. That doesn't mean we shouldn't set goals. If we do not know what we want, that is okay. We already learned how to cultivate more energy, so now we at least have more energy to go out and try new things. We might find something we like, but we will definitely find things we do not like, which is just as important.

In order to create all of our desires, we must first figure out what we want. This is the hardest part about getting started. A dream is a goal that is written down. If we never write anything down, it only exists in our head. If it exists in our head, it doesn't exist at all.

Our goals are not written in stone. We are allowed to change them. The power is in writing down your dreams and putting a timeline to them.

That is a true goal: a dream that is written down with an end date. Just the act of doing this sends our brain into problem-solving mode. It will try to find ways to make this happen. The more you write down your goals and say them out loud to yourself, the more your subconscious mind starts to create them.

Think of a time when you wanted to buy a car. Say you wanted to get a red Ferrari. You think about it all day, about how great it would be to have one. Then, what happens? Later that day, you see a red Ferrari driving around!

Our subconscious is really good at creating. We just have to get specific with what we want.

I know this all too well.

I wanted to coach Olympians. I was not specific enough, so I got to train beach volleyball players and then ski halfpipe.

Whatever we think about, we create. If we never put it down on paper and get specific about it, it never happens.

Apply: Don't just write goals; create an identity.

Who do you need to be to make this happen? Then, envision yourself already being this person. You start showing up as this person each and every day.

Goal setting->mantras->identity

"The difference between a dream and a goal is that a goal is written down."

–Mark England

When we write our goals in a different manner, things in our life begin to rearrange, and they become much more achievable much more quickly.

Oftentimes, we set goals that are not our own. We look at others' goals and think we want that, as well. We need to do the work and figure out what goals *we* want to reach and what processes *we* need to put into place to become that person who achieves these types of goals.

The following is an example of how I set goals for myself to become a bestselling author and write this book. I did not just sit down one day and write this book. I started by writing down my goal like this:

1.   Set goal:

"I want_____, because_____."

"I want to become a bestselling author because I want to teach people how to grow their capacity through confidence to live their dream life."

Start by using this "I want to_____, because_____," framework. Then we can focus on changing our identity to become the person we need to be to accomplish this goal. So, we begin to show up as that person every day, as if we already have completed it. Results do not matter. What matters is how we show up every day!

2.   Change Identity:

Put yourself in persona of the person you need to be, or any other way you need, in order to reach your goal.

Be as specific as you can. What does that look like in your life?

Anywhere you can get more accurate, do it. Accuracy is key. Be very specific.

➢   How do you show up every day?
➢   For you to create this, how do you need to show up in the world?

Then make it present tense.

So, my goal changed to:

"By November 2019, I become a bestselling author, because I want to help teach people how to grow their capacity through confidence to create the life of their dreams and to live their perfect day every day."

Then I added who I needed to be (in present tense) or to show up as every day, to reach this goal.

- ➤ I am a bestselling author.
- ➤ I am an incredible storyteller.
- ➤ I am impeccable with my words.
- ➤ I inspire my readers to take action.
- ➤ My readers receive extraordinary results.
- ➤ I create cognitive shifts required to change my behavior.
- ➤ My readers value their process for finding confidence.
- ➤ I am confident.
- ➤ I am patient.
- ➤ I am enough.
- ➤ I am complete.

Write down all of the things you think you need to be and the things that feel good, when you say them.

3. Connect breath to mantras:

This is where the magic happens. Every morning, when I get up, I read my goals and my mantras out loud to myself. Every morning and night, I put my attention to who I need to show up as every day.

Just like thinking about wanting a red Ferrari and then seeing one later that day, I prime my body by affirming who I need to be to reach my goals. Then my body starts to become that person, and my goals just start happening for me. That's why you are reading this book currently!

The real magic starts to happen when you add your breath. Remember, we can use our breath to down-regulate ourselves. Using a longer exhale than inhale lets us get to that parasympathetic state, where our body is much more open to opportunity.

In a way, your body (nervous system) might be rejecting goals.

Adding breathwork down-regulates you and makes you more open to receive this new identity. We must let go of our old identity to become this new person.

Get comfortable with verbalizing what you want. Our own voice sounds strange. Get comfortable hearing yourself speak. Watch yourself in a mirror.

Say it with confidence. When it starts to get smooth, you are showing up as that person every day.

4.   Create your story:

We are the authors of our own story. Our days begin and end as stories. Spend some time each morning and night telling yourself what your story is. The more you do it, the more you start to believe it.

5.   Breathe into your Goals/Mantras/Identity technique:

➤   Write down a specific goal/mantra/ identity

➤   Read goal out loud

➤   Re-read goal out loud again, this time at a smooth, relaxed pace

➤   Read again, but pause at end of each sentence and inhale for four seconds, exhale for eight seconds (down-regulate).

This process only takes a few minutes each day, but it is incredibly powerful. When I sit down in the morning to do it, I feel ready to take on the world and achieve my goals, because I know I am showing up as that person each and every day.

I repeat this same process with all of my goals.

Once a week, I will spend fifteen to twenty minutes reading and saying out loud all of my goals and mantras. Every morning, I usually choose one or two goals and sets of mantras that feel important to me that day.

For example, say one morning I am feeling stressed about my finances. I will then focus my mantras that day on my financial goals and my money mantras. Doing this then makes me feel less stressed about my finances that day, because I know I have my processes running and they are taking care of it, so I do not have to stress out about it and let it affect my entire day.

Having a breathwork and mantra practice is just a way of reminding you each day of what is important, so that, as the day goes on and we get tired and stressed out, we still make better decisions because we have reminded ourself of who we need to be each day in order to keep growing our capacity and confidence.

This practice builds confidence.

Confidence comes from little wins each day. If all I do is read my goals and mantras, that is a win for the day. We want to celebrate wins. Wins build momentum. Momentum builds confidence. Confidence lets us build the life of our dreams.

Confidence is a process. It is unique to everyone. Everyone has bad days sure. Successful people have spent time on developing their processes so well that their process doesn't allow them to have two bad days in a row. Because momentum can also work the other way.

We want to have a process that we have confidence in. Our process is always evolving and ever-changing. We just keep working on it. Programs start and stop, but processes are always running.

When we have a good process and we enjoy our process, the results don't matter. We cannot control the results. It can rain. We can miss our flight. The referee can make a bad call. We cannot control it. So, the only thing we can do is control what we can control. If we take ownership of our process and enjoy our process, then the results will not matter because we enjoyed the ride to get where we are now.

If we do not like the process, then we will not like the result.

That is the untold secret of the fitness industry. You have to take care of yourself. You have to develop you own processes. Doctors and lifeguards are there to save you in case of emergency only. We are responsible for taking care of our own health wealth and happiness.

This book is for me, too. To remind me to always keep working on my process. It is an infinite process, but it is mine, and I enjoy it. It allows me to always keep increasing my capacity to evolve to the next level of this human experience.

CHAPTER 6

BUILDING A CONFIDENCE PROCESS

Care: Take care of yourself

IT IS THE RESPONSIBILITY of each one of us to care for ourselves. Doctors and lifeguards are there in case of emergency only. The rest of the time, it is your responsibility to take ownership of your health and wellbeing. We cannot help others if we cannot take care of ourselves.

We want to fill others from a cup that is overflowing. This book hopefully has given you some strategies, so you can begin to find ways to cultivate more energy and fill yourself up first. We have to be incredibly selfish with our time and energy. People are always going to take and want more from us. We have to learn to set boundaries and protect ourselves.

This is the most important lesson in the book. In order to be self-less, we must be selfish. In order to become the person we know we can become, we must learn to invest in ourselves.

In this teach section, I am going to introduce my mentors. We cannot do anything great alone. We need others to help us see our limitations. The only limitations we have are the ones we place on ourselves. We tend to look at ourselves with rose-colored glasses, which makes it difficult to see what is holding us back.

I invested nine years of my coaching career in going as far as I could on my own. I became an incredible coach. However, as you learned in this book, I reached a point where I didn't want to do it anymore. I was tired of always giving to everyone else.

I have always preached that everyone needs a coach. Nine years into my career, I figured it was finally time to invest in myself and hire mentors, people who were the best of the best in their fields, to get me to where I wanted to go.

It was incredibly expensive, but the more you pay, the more you pay attention. Looking back at how my mentors have helped me remove my limiting beliefs, build my process, and hold me accountable to what I said I was going to do, I would have paid them way more. Coaches/mentors are the stewards of the client's dreams.

My mentors and coaches guided me to my greatness and allowed me to find joy again, which allowed me to create my perfect day every day!

Teach: Carl Paoli

This right here is an incredible human. All of my friends have amazing stories to tell about him. Carl has not just inspired me but hundreds of thousands of people all over the world to be better movers.

Carl might have been the first person to say that performance is a feeling. This was a game-changer for me. It shifted the way I thought about performance and fitness.

I first found Carl like everyone else did: on Gymnastics WOD. Through posting his videos online, Carl taught most of the CrossFit coaches how to coach gymnastics.

Being a former high-level gymnast himself (an alternate for the Spanish Olympic team), he breaks down and explains movement better than anyone I know. He does this so well that he wrote a book about it: *FreeStyle*. He now tours the world spreading his message. His book is the backbone for breaking down any movement into a progression that can be scaled, so anyone of any ability can learn any movements, from the most basic to the most complex.

I learned how to be a better coach from watching his videos. I would watch his videos and then go and try the progressions.

I was filling in at a CrossFit box one time, and it had rope climbs in the workout. I had never done a rope climb before, so, I pulled up Carl's progressions on how to climb a rope. I watched them, I went and tried them, and I climbed a rope for the first time. Then I went and taught a class on how to rope climb. No one knew it was my first time climbing a rope!

That is a great example of how a coach can guide you to do things you never thought you could do. But we all have to actually go out and *do* these things, not just watch the video.

I started working with Carl many years later. He was offering lifestyle design. He was teaching people how to design their lives to create the life of their dreams. I had always looked up to Carl, so I applied. This was one of the hardest things I ever had to do.

A day later, I got a message back from Carl's wife saying Carl was so excited to work with me. *What*?! One of the people whom I considered one of my heroes was excited to work with *me,* because he thought what *I* was doing was cool?? Amazing!

Working with Carl helped me work through a framework of how to design my dream life, including the action steps to make it happen. As you learned earlier, he was also the person to tell me exactly what I needed to hear when I was in a horrible place in life. That's what coaches do. They tell you what you need to hear, even if it is not what we want to hear.

Teach: AJ Mihrzad, the online super coach.

AJ is the reason you are all reading this book right now. In fact, I am sitting in his backyard writing this book currently.

I hired AJ to teach me how to create an online coaching business. I got way more than that. AJ showed me his process of how to create an online business, so I could serve more people. I was nine years into the coaching game and was tired of trading hours for dollars. I could only work with so many people in person, and there were so many more people whom I could help. AJ was the coach I hired. He was so expensive, I had to take out a loan. I had to put some skin in the game. I had to be all-in.

Through AJ's program, I gained confidence in my abilities, because I followed his program exactly and got the exact results he promised. This shot my confidence through the roof. All he did was give me the program and, each week, hold me accountable for what I said I was going to do.

What I needed to do was to get uncomfortable. I was comfortable. He made me step outside my comfort zone, so I could really step into my full potential. I learned from him that fear and discomfort were things I needed, in order to keep growing, and if I was going to help my clients get over fear and discomfort, I sure as shit better be doing the same.

Teach: The Strong Coach program—Mike Bledsoe and Daniel Rios

Mike Bledsoe was, in many ways, like Carl Paoli for me. He created the *Barbell Shrugged* podcast, a podcast for strength and conditioning pros to learn everything they needed to know about anything strength and conditioning.

Barbell Shrugged was my go-to resource for continuing education for CrossFit, as well as strength and conditioning.

Then, he created the Strong Coach program, which is a twelve-week program that I completed. This program changed my life.

I knew I was destined for greatness, but I had never defined it. I guess I sort of just thought I would arrive there one day. This self-development program forced me to sit down with myself and put effort into writing specific goals. And not just specific goals but *unreasonably* specific goals.

I stole Mike's goal of wanting to heal the fitness industry. I agreed it was broken and not serving anyone anymore. This class helped me get clear on my goals and become really specific. Once I did that, I started reaching goals faster than I ever could have imagined.

They say you are the sum of the five people you spend the most time with. Well, I have been spending some time with some pretty awesome people, who have all guided me to my greatness. They saw it in me. Then I had to see it and experience it for myself.

It is one thing to hire mentors to tell you what you need to do. You still have to put in the work. Mentors can only guide you. You have to lead the way.

Train: Everyone needs a coach

Now, I know that getting a coach or a mentor might not be in everyone's budget, and that is okay. For nine years, I worked as a coach on my own and I reached a very high level. I would even call myself a master coach.

How did I get there: FITOY.

> ➢ Figure
> ➢ IT
> ➢ Out
> ➢ Yourself

You still have to do the work. No one is going to do it for you. All of these programs and processes give to me by my mentors only worked because I had already tried everything else on my own.

This is the problem with the fitness industry, as well. We let our coaches and trainers become a crutch. We rely on them to do everything for us. What happens once we stop working with our coaches? Do we continue to see results? Or do we fall back into our same-old bad habits and routines?

We have to learn to take what others have done, and see it for what it is. Take what we like, and get rid of what we don't, then come up with our own unique process. This process is what is going to keep bringing you success.

Programs start and stop. Processes are always going. They are there to catch you when you have a bad day. Processes are there to make sure you do not have two bad days in a row.

My Gift to You!

I WANT TO GIVE you a gift.

I am offering you a free 8-Day Cognitive Shift Process to Creating More Capacity Through Confidence, to thank you for reading this book. It will show you how to put into action some of the strategies that have worked for me.

All you need to do is email me here:

KennyKallenCoach@gmail.com

I will respond by emailing you back the program. Please download and try it out. Then let me know what you think about it!

I know it will inspire you create your own process for creating wins, building momentum, and growing confidence to create the life of your dreams.

Also, please visit my website:

www.optimizedlifestylecoaching.com

There you can sign-up for my newsletter, where I offer you regular ongoing health, nutrition, workout tips, along with encouragement, wisdom, and community. When you subscribe to my content, the energy and benefits of this book will continue to ripple out to you and your future endeavors, allowing you to keep developing and refining your process. Check it out now!

Also, please join my Facebook page and share your experiences creating your process, as you develop it using this book. I would love to see you post your successes on my wall:

www.facebook.com/profile.php?id=10037050

And guess what? You can *hire me*!

Humans need help to see our limitations. The only limits are the ones we place on ourselves.

I have clients all over the world. Send me an email for some special information on my services, and let me help you even more to dial in your confidence process.

Kenny@optimizedlifestylecoaching.com

ABOUT KENNY

KENNY KALLEN is a lifelong athlete and competitor with a huge passion for coaching and teaching. He currently lives in Santa Monica with his wife and cat, Asha. He has a private coaching practice plus teaches at the National Personal Training Institute, teaching the NASM Certified Personal Trainer Course, and other advanced courses.

He graduated from Arizona State University with a B.S. in kinesiology. Since then, he has worked extensively with professional, collegiate, and Olympic athletes, as well as a broad range of everyday fitness enthusiasts who range from four- to eighty-year-olds. He has experience both coaching and competing in Olympic lifting, powerlifting, and CrossFit, and has even run a marathon.

Kenny coached for Velocity Sports Performance for almost a decade, helping young athletes become stronger and faster for their sport. In his time at Velocity, he also worked with many National Olympic teams, and he traveled the world as the Fitness Coach for the Chinese National Ski Halfpipe team, preparing for the 2022 Beijing Olympics.

There are few professionals in the field more dedicated, hardworking, and passionate about helping to improve performance and the overall lives of others. Kenny's athletes and students feel inspired, motivated, and excited about coming to class every day. He makes the learning fun, engaging, and challenging, while continuously seeking to improve everyone's experience and create an optimum learning environment for all.

Kenny wants to transform the fitness industry. He guides his students and athletes to achieve their inherent greatness and unlimited potential.

His Motto: Using science, intuition, and joy to combat stress and increase energy, efficiency, creativity, focus, adaptation, and motivation.

Build your process for confidence, so you can live your perfect day every day.

His certificates and achievements include:

- B.S. kinesiology, Arizona State University
- NASM Certified Personal Trainer *with distinction
- NASM Performance Enhancement Specialist
- NSCA Certified Strength & Conditioning Coach
- CrossFit L1 Trainer
- CrossFit Football Certified